DREAM BIG & BELIEVE IN YOURSELF

"I can do all things through Christ which strengtheneth me."

PHILIPPIANS 4:13

by

Franklin N. Abazie

Dream Big & believe in your self
COPYRIGHT 2019 *by* Franklin N Abazie
ISBN: ISBN: 978-1-945-133-59-6

All right reserved. This book or any portion thereof may not be reproduced or used in any manner whatsoever without the express written permission of the publisher, except for the use of brief quotations in a book review. All Bible quotes are from King James Version and others as noted.

Published by:
F N ABAZIE PUBLISHING HOUSE---a.k.a,
Empowerment Bookstore:

That I may publish with the voice of thanksgiving and tell of all thy wondrous works.
Psalms26:7

To order additional copies, wholesales or booking:
Call the Church office (973-372-7518)
or Empowerment Bookstore Hotline 973-393-8518

Worship address:
343 Sanford Avenue Newark New Jersey 07106
Administrative Head Office address:
33 Schley Street Newark New Jersey 07112
Email:pastorfranknto@yahoo.com
Website www.fnabaziehealingministries.org
Publishing House: www.fnabaziepublishinghouse.org

This book is a production of F N Abazie Publishing House. A publication Arms of Miracle of God Ministries 2019
First Edition

CONTENTS

The Mandate of The Commission iv

Favor Confession vi

Introduction viii

CHAPTER 1
The Power of a Positive Attitude 38

CHAPTER 2
The Power of a Big Dream 50

CHAPTER 3
Prayer of Salvation 69

CHAPTER 4
About The Author 79

Books By Rev Franklin N Abazie 81

Dream Big & Believe in Yourself

THE MANDATE OF THE COMMISSION

"THE MOMENT IS DUE TO IMPACT YOUR WORLD THROUGH THE REVIVAL OF THE HEALING & MIRACLE MINISTRY OF JESUS CHRIST OF NAZARETH."

"I AM SENDING YOU TO RESTORE HEALTH UNTO THEE AND I WILL HEAL THEE OF THY WOUNDS, SAID THE LORD OF HOST."

ARMS OF THE COMMISSION

1) F N Abazie Ministries-Miracle of God Ministries (Miracle Chapel Intl)
2) F N Abazie TV Ministries: Global Television Ministry Outreach.
3) F N Abazie Radio Ministries: Radio Broadcasting Outreach.
4) F N Abazie Publishing House: Book Publication.
5) F N Abazie Bible School: also called Word of Healing Bible School (W.O.H.B.S)
6) F N Abazie Evangelistic Ass: Miracle of God Ministries: Global Crusade
7) Empowerment Bookstore: Book distribution.
8) F N Abazie Helping Hands: Meeting the help of the needy world wide
9) F N Abazie Disaster Recovery Mission: Global Disaster Recovery.
10) F N Abazie Prison Ministry: Prison Ministry for all convicts "Second chance"

Some of our ministry arms are waiting the appointed time to commence.

Dream Big & Believe in Yourself

FAVOR CONFESSION

Father thank you for making me righteous and accepted through the blood of Jesus Christ. Because of that, I am blessed and highly favored by God. I am the subject of your affection. Your favor surrounds me as a shield, and the first thing that people see around me is your favored shield.

Thank you that I have favor with you and man today. All day long people go out of their way to bless me and help me. I have favor with everyone that I deal with today. Doors that were once closed are now opened for me. I receive preferential treatment, and I have special privileges, I am Gods favored child.

No good thing will he withhold from me. Because of Gods favor my enemies cannot triumph over my life. I have supernatural increase and promotion. I declare restoration to everything that the devil has stolen

Favor Confession

from my life. I have honor in the midst of my adversaries and an increase in assets, especially in real estate and expansion of territories.

Because I am highly favored by God, I experience great victories, supernatural turnarounds, and miraculous breakthrough in the midst of great impossibilities. I receive recognition, prominence, and honor. Petitions are granted to me even by ungodly authorities. Policies, rules, regulations, and laws are changed and reverse on my behalf.

I win battles that I don't even have to fight, because God fights them for me. This is the day, the set time and the designated moment for me to experience the free favor of God, that profusely and lavishly abound on my behalf in Jesus name. **Amen.**

INTRODUCTION

A dream doesn't become reality through magic; it takes sweat, determination, and hard work.

Collin Powel

I may never get to meet with you in my life time. *But thanks be to God who gave us wisdom* to write and print books for people like you. My sole reason to write this small book is for you to take action concerning your dreams and visions.

I am *absolutely sure that God spoke to you so many years ago, or even recently about your future and your dream*. Your goals and dreams will remain dormant unless, you do something about it.

I *came to encourage you, I came to assist you through the instructions and*

Introduction

relevant information's, in this book to take quick action. I have continued to take action in my life, regardless of the size. I am literally doing what am called to do in my life time. *I preach, I write, and pray for a lot of people all over the world.* It is my heaven assignment-which I have embraced with joy into my life.

Some of these people we follow in life are common people that took *uncommon action in their life.* I want you to also join us and take *action in your own life.* I do not have the details of the area where God have called you. But I am absolutely sure that *God have an assignment* for you.

Rome they said was not built in one day. There is a reason why you are here. *Find out what has been missing in your life by taking accurate action about it.* Therefore as you read this small book, *plan, prepare, and execute definite action to confirm that you got something out of this small book.* Relax and let here what the Holy Spirit is saying in this book.

Happy reading!

HIS DESTINY WAS THE CROSS....

HIS PURPOSE WAS LOVE....

HIS REASON WAS YOU....

"Whoever loves discipline loves knowledge, but he who hates reproof is stupid."

Proverb12:1

As many as I love, I rebuke and chasten: be zealous therefore, and repent.

Rev 3:19

"I therefore so run, not as uncertainly; so fight I, not as one that beateth the air:"

1cor9:26

"But I keep under my body, and bring it into subjection: lest that by any means, when I have preached to others, I myself should be a castaway."

1cor9:27

"I must work the works of him that sent me, while it is day: the night cometh, when no man can work."

John9:4

"Whoever spares the rod hates his son, but he who loves him is diligent to discipline him."

Proverb13:24

> *"Those whom I love, I reprove and discipline, so be zealous and repent."*
>
> **Revelation 3:19**

"The rod and reproof give wisdom, but a child left to himself brings shame to his mother."

Proverb29:15

"So he fed them according to the integrity of his heart; and guided them by the skilfulness of his hands."

Psalm 78:72

"And ye have forgotten the exhortation which speaketh unto you as unto children, My son, despise not thou the chastening of the Lord, nor faint when thou art rebuked of him:"

Hebrews12:5

"For whom the Lord loveth he chasteneth, and scourgeth every son whom he receiveth."

Hebrews12:6

"If ye endure chastening, God dealeth with you as with sons; for what son is he whom the father chasteneth not"?

Hebrews12:7

"But if ye be without chastisement, whereof all are partakers, then are ye bastards, and not sons."

Hebrews12:8

"Furthermore we have had fathers of our flesh which corrected us, and we gave them reverence: shall we not much rather be in subjection unto the Father of spirits, and live?"

Hebrews 12:9

"He that spareth his rod hateth his son: but he that loveth him chasteneth him betimes."

Proverb13:24

"Let thy work appear unto thy servants, and thy glory unto their children."

Psalm 90:16

"And let the beauty of the Lord our God be upon us: and establish thou the work of our hands upon us; yea, the work of our hands establish thou it."

Psalm 90:17

"And he shall be like a tree planted by the rivers of water, that bringeth forth his fruit in his season; his leaf also shall not wither; and whatsoever he doeth shall prosper."

Psalm1:3

"I must work the works of him that sent me, while it is day: the night cometh, when no man can work."

John9:4

xxx

"For even when we were with you, this we commanded you, that if any would not work, neither should he eat."

2theo3:10

"And that ye study to be quiet, and to do your own business, and to work with your own hands, as we commanded you;

1theo4:11

"To discipline a child produces wisdom, but a mother is disgraced by an undisciplined child."

Proverbs 29:15

"Whoever loves discipline loves knowledge, but whoever hates correction is stupid."

Proverbs 12:1

"Blessed is the one whom God corrects; so do not despise the discipline of the Almighty."

Job 5:17

> "Blessed is the one you discipline, LORD, the one you teach from your law;"

Psalm 94:12

But Jesus answered them, My Father worketh hitherto, and I work.

John5:17

CHAPTER 1
THE POWER OF A POSITIVE ATTITUDE

"And she said, Let thine handmaid find grace in thy sight. So the woman went her way, and did eat, and her countenance was no more sad."

1 Samuel 1:18

For unless *we maintain a positive attitude in life, the world system is designed to operate against us*. Even when you try and fail in life, I indulge you to, *never give up*. **"For quitters never win"** If you must become *successful in life, you must embrace the spirit of endurance.*

In my opinion, a positive attitude is all it takes to overcome trials and tribulation in

CHAPTER 1 : The Power of a Positive Attitude

life. Therefore put your attitude together and launch a comeback against that set back.

*"These things I have spoken unto you, that in me ye might have peace. In the world ye shall have tribulation: but be of good cheer; I have overcome the world."***John16:33**

A positive attitude towards your dream is all it takes to launch a comeback.

Just the fact that you tried and failed does not excuse you from trying again. I am a living witness of trying and failing in life, yet I keep going forward doing what God has called me to do. I do all these, because I have *faith in God* and I *believe in myself*.

Leah Labelle said.....

"Work hard for what you want because it won't come to you without a fight. You have to be strong and courageous and know that you can do anything you put your mind to. If somebody puts you down or criticizes you, just keep on believing in yourself and turn it into something positive." –**Leah Labelle**

Tena Desae once said…

"Stay positive and happy. Work hard and don't give up hope. Be open to criticism and keep learning. Surround yourself with happy, warm and genuine people." - **Tena Desae**

Here this …….

"For a just man falleth seven times, and riseth up again: but the wicked shall fall into mischief." **Proverb24:16**

"Though he fall, he shall not be utterly cast down: for the Lord upholdeth him with his hand." **Psalm37:24**

"My flesh and my heart faileth: but God is the strength of my heart, and my portion for ever." **Psalm73:26**

CHAPTER 1 : The Power of a Positive Attitude

"No, I tell you; but unless you repent, you will all likewise perish." **Luke13:3**

"Bear fruit in keeping with repentance." **Mathew3:8**

Colin Powell once said and I quote…..

"A dream doesn't become reality through magic; it takes sweat, determination and hard work."- **Colin Powell**

Gail Devers went further to say….

"Keep your dreams alive. Understand to achieve anything requires faith and belief in yourself, vision, hard work, determination, and dedication. Remember all things are possible for those who believe. Gail Devers."-**Gail Devers**

In my 45 years on earth, I have never seen anyone or any family that hates success. My bible says *wealth has many friends.* If you must succeed, you must work hard, and maintain a positive attitude in life. You will agree with me that we all want to succeed in life, but we lack the mental attitude to overcome trial and temptation of life.

Here this….

"Success is no accident. It is hard work, perseverance, learning, studying, sacrifice and most of all, love of what you are doing or learning to do." **–Pele**

The bible says *"many are called but few are chosen"*. If you must impact your world you must embrace the power of a positive attitude.

One great philosopher once said ……

"Luck is great, but most of life is hard work."

To believe in yourself is an *expression of our faith in Christ Jesus*. Jesus said

CHAPTER 1 : The Power of a Positive Attitude

"As soon as Jesus heard the word that was spoken, he saith unto the ruler of the synagogue, Be not afraid, only believe." **Mark5:36**

"But when Jesus heard it, he answered him, saying, Fear not: believe only, and she shall be made whole." **Luke8:50**

"Verily, verily, I say unto you, He that believeth on me, the works that I do shall he do also; and greater works than these shall he do; because I go unto my Father." **John14:12**

Every Christian is supposed to make greater impact in life. If you are not making impact then you are spiritually dead. There must be a greater reason for your living. *Have you ever asked why you are alive? Or why are you here?*

You are here to make greater impact in the lives of others. God is looking at your attitude. Often God will allow you to fail or go through challenges in life. *But it's only a test of your faith.* Job said "...when he hath tried me, I shall come forth as gold". **Job23:10**

Your positive attitude is the primary catalyst to win in life. To become successful in life, you must *Dream big and believe in yourself.*

"I can do all things through Christ which strengthened me." **Phil4:13**

As long as you set your mind on your assignment God will make it happen for you. *Have you discovered your assignment on earth?* God want to bless your life, but you need to find your assignment. God does not bless anyone without a dream and without a job. God blesses the work of your hand.

"And let the beauty of the Lord our God be upon us: and establish thou the work of

CHAPTER 1 : The Power of a Positive Attitude

our hands upon us; yea, the work of our hands establish thou it." **Psalm90:17**

"And he shall be like a tree planted by the rivers of water, that bringeth forth his fruit in his season; his leaf also shall not wither; and whatsoever he doeth shall prosper." **Psalm1:3**

The above underlined scripture above says, I can do all things through Christ which strengthens me. *Through Christ means you must have faith in God and in yourself.*

If you can change the way you think, the way you handle money, the way you plan, prepare and execute your current assignment. God will honor your life. You see; God is looking for how you handle the challenges that come to you now. If you can handle it properly then you are ready for your next level in life.

YOU MUST PLAN YOUR LIFE

"For I would that all men were even as I myself. But every man hath his proper gift of God, one after this manner, and another after that." **1 cor7:7**

"But as God hath distributed to every man, as the Lord hath called every one, so let him walk. And so ordain I in all churches." **1cor7:17**

"Let every man abide in the same calling wherein he was called." **1cor7:20**

"Brethren, let every man, wherein he is called, therein abide with God." **1cor7:24**

I have seen a lot of people jump from one trade to the next, from one discipline to the next. If you keep jumping from car sales man to a real estate agent and from a real estate agent to a day trader. *How can God bless your life?*

CHAPTER 1 : The Power of a Positive Attitude

I pray you locate your God given assignment before it's too late for you in life. You must plan your life. You do not have the luxury to toy around with your time. Your time is your greatest investment in life.

WE ARE COMMANDED….

"Delight thyself also in the Lord: and he shall give thee the desires of thine heart." **Psalm37:4**

"For where your treasure is, there will your heart be also." **Mathew6:21**

Accept yourself for who you are. Embrace your personality. Never play the blame game. You are not cursed, you are blessed. There is something greater inside of you that is invisible. *"greater is he that is in you, than he that is in the world."*

ALWAYS WRITE OUT YOUR GOALS AND PLAN

"For which of you, intending to build a tower, sitteth not down first, and counteth the cost, whether he have sufficient to finish it?" **Luke 14:28**

The pursuit of your *dreams* begins in the mind, *an act of faith* combined *with a giant act of will*. But when it pays off, it becomes a reality- if am permitted to call it *a testimony*. I would argue with you that having a big dream in life takes *courage* and *faith. If you can dare to believe in God and in yourself. God will make His word good towards you.*

YOUR BREAKTHROUGH IS IN YOUR DECISION.

I heard a preacher say one time in 2006 that the decision you take today, will determine the future you will create.

CHAPTER 1 : The Power of a Positive Attitude

Will you take a decision today concerning your future?

"There is a way that seemeth right unto a man, but the end thereof are the ways of death." **Proverb16:25**

"There is a way which seemeth right unto a man, but the end thereof are the ways of death." **Proverb14:12**

Cultivate a positive attitude. Success is the product of your faith. Have faith in God and pursue your God given dream in life.

CHAPTER 2
THE POWER OF A BIG DREAM

"Now unto him that is able to do exceeding abundantly above all that we ask or think, according to the power that worketh in us,"
Ephesians 3:20

"Neither shall they say, Lo here! or, lo there! for, behold, the kingdom of God is within you." **Luke 17:21**

"And Joseph dreamed a dream, and he told it his brethren: and they hated him yet the more." **Genesis 37:5**

"For God speaketh once, yea twice, yet man perceiveth it not. In a dream, in a vision of the night, when deep sleep falleth upon men, in slumberings upon the bed; Then he

CHAPTER 2 : The Power of a Big Dream

openeth the ears of men, and sealeth their instruction." **Job33:14-16**

"For I am the Lord: I will speak, and the word that I shall speak shall come to pass; it shall be no more prolonged: for in your days, O rebellious house, will I say the word, and will perform it, saith the Lord God." **Ezekiel12:25**

"Therefore say unto them, Thus saith the Lord God; There shall none of my words be prolonged any more, but the word which I have spoken shall be done, saith the Lord God." **Ezekiel12:28**

If you can think big, dream big, God will make it happen in your life time. Impact is all about touching lives. *"Who is he that saith, and it cometh to pass, when the Lord commandeth it not?"*

We must always allow God to lead us in life. Whenever you lead yourself you are heading into destruction. *For as many as are led by the Spirit of God, they are the sons of God.*

God speak through our dream.

"And Pharaoh said unto Joseph, I have dreamed a dream, and there is none that can interpret it: and I have heard say of thee, that thou canst understand a dream to interpret it. **Genesis41:15**

The Spirit itself beareth witness with our spirit, that we are the children of God: **Romans8:16**

And Joseph answered Pharaoh, saying, It is not in me: God shall give Pharaoh an answer of peace." **Genesis41:16**

God will always give you a dream, but it's up to you to follow it or to abandon it in life.

CHAPTER 2 : The Power of a Big Dream

HINDRANCE TO YOUR DREAM

-----Fear of uncertainty-----

A lot of folks will never try anything new in life. "*As long as you over analyze, you will paralyze*" God said for you to take action. **Your waiting season is over.**

-----Wrong association-----

Who are your friends…?

Show me your friends and I will show you your future. We were told *Make no friendship with an angry man; and with a furious man thou shalt not go".* **Proverb22:25**

-----Negative mindset-----

"And be renewed in the spirit of your mind" **Ephesians4:23.**

If you do not have a dream yet? It means you have not been thinking right. If you can change the way you think, God will bless your life supernaturally.

-----Doubt-----

You must *dream big* and *believe in yourself*. Doubt is designed to keep us stranded in life *"A double minded man is unstable in all his ways."* **James1:8**

If you are still doubting-it means you are living an unstable lifestyle. If you can *dream big* and *believe in yourself,* God will make it happen in your life. If you are realistic about your present condition and do something positive about it. God will grant you favor to accomplish it.

"Thou openest thine hand, and satisfiest the desire of every living thing." **Psalm145:16**

"The Lord upholdeth all that fall, and raiseth up all those that be bowed down." **Psalm145:14**

CHAPTER 2 : The Power of a Big Dream

"The eyes of all wait upon thee; and thou givest them their meat in due season."
Psalm 145:15

Therefore I encourage you to keep dreaming. Keep your head's up, there is light at the end of the tunnel. If you fail, rise up and dusk up yourself. Try again, keep on trying you will eventually succeed in life. I see you succeeding in the midst of the challenges of life.

SUCCESS STORIES OF SIX KNOWN PEOPLE TO ENCOURAGE YOU

In my opinion I define failure as …

F   FIRST

A   ATTEMPT

I   IN

L   LEARNING

The fact that you tried before and failed does not mean you should quit. *"Winners do not quit and quitter never win in life"*. In fact failure is a boaster of your *faith in God. Do you believe in God? Do you believe in yourself?*

In my opinion *failure is not the alternative to success.* It's only a temporary setback in my own definition for a greater comeback that will usher in a more impactful and successful future. *Everybody encounters failure at one point or another*. The important characteristics is how you react to and learn from that failure.

The stories of these six entrepreneurs. Their stories ended into a global success, but all of them went through failure and difficulty at one point in their lives. They are perfect examples of a big dream come true. That is why failure should never stop anyone from dreaming in life.

CHAPTER 2 : The Power of a Big Dream

1. Arianna Huffington got rejected by 36 publishers.

It's hard to believe that one of the most recognizable names in online publications was once rejected by three dozen major publishers. Huffington's second book, which she tried to publish long before she created the now ubiquitously recognizable Huffington Post Empire, was rejected 36 times before it was eventually accepted for publication.

Barbara Corcoran:
Failure Is My Specialty

Even Huffington Post itself wasn't a success right away. In fact, when it launched, there were dozens of highly negative reviews about its quality and it's potential. Obviously, Huffington overcame those initial bouts of failure and has cemented her name as one of the most successful outlets on the web.

2. Bill Gates watched his first company crumble.

Bill Gates is now one of the world's wealthiest individuals, but he didn't earn his fortune overnight. Bill Gates entered the entrepreneurial scene with a company called *Traf-O-Data,* which aimed to process and analyze the data from traffic tapes (think of it like an early version of big data). He tried to sell the idea alongside his business partner, Paul Allen, but the product barely even worked. It was a complete disaster. However, the failure did not hold Gates back from exploring new opportunities, and a few years later, he created his first Microsoft product, and forged a new path to success.

3. George Steinbrenner bankrupted a team.

Before Steinbrenner made a name for himself when he acquired ownership of the New York Yankees, he owned a small

CHAPTER 2 : The Power of a Big Dream

basketball team called the Cleveland Pipers back in 1960. By 1962, as a result of Steinbrenner's direction, the entire franchise went bankrupt.

That stretch of failure seemed to follow Steinbrenner when he took over the Yankees in the 1970s, as the team struggled with a number of setbacks and losses throughout the 1980s and 1990s. However, despite public fear and criticism of Steinbrenner's controversial decisions, eventually he led the team to an amazing comeback, with six World Series entries between 1996 and 2003, and a record as one of the most profitable teams in Major League Baseball.

Related: To Manage Innovation, Manage Failure Better

4. Walt Disney was told he lacked creativity.

One of the most creative geniuses of the 20th century was once fired from a newspaper because he was told he lacked creativity. Trying to persevere, Disney formed his first animation company, which was called *Laugh-O-Gram Films*. He *raised $15,000 for the company but eventually was forced to close Laugh-O-Gram,* following the close of an important distributor partner. *Desperate and out of money, Disney found his way to Hollywood and faced even more criticism and failure until finally, his first few classic films started to skyrocket in popularity.*

5. Steve Jobs was booted from his own company.

Steve Jobs is an impressive entrepreneur because of his boundless innovations, but also because of his emphatic comeback from an almost irrecoverable failure. Jobs found success in his 20s when Apple became a massive empire, but when he was 30, Apple's board of directors decided

CHAPTER 2 : The Power of a Big Dream

to fire him. Undaunted by the failure, Jobs founded a new company, NEXT, which was eventually acquired by Apple. Once back at Apple, Jobs proved his capacity for greatness by reinventing the company's image and taking the Apple brand to new heights.

6. Milton Hershey started three candy companies before Hershey's.

Everyone knows Hershey's chocolate, but when Milton Hershey first started his candy production career, he was a-nobody. After being fired from an apprenticeship with a printer, Hershey started three separate candy-related ventures, and was forced to watch all of them fail. In one last attempt, Hershey founded the Lancaster Caramel Company, and started seeing enormous results. Believing in his vision for milk chocolate for the masses, he eventually founded the Hershey Company and became one of the most well-known names in the industry.

I therefore encourage you to draw inspiration from these stories the next time you experience failure, no matter the scale. In the moment, some failure might seem like the end of the road, but remember, there are countless successful men and women in the world today who are only enjoying success because they decided to push past the inevitable bleakness of failure. Learn from your mistakes, reflect and accept the failure, but revisit your passion and keep pursuing your dreams no matter what.

CHAPTER 2 : The Power of a Big Dream

I WANT TO HEAR FROM YOU. PLEASE TAKE TIME TO WRITE ME BACK

Rev Franklin N Abazie
33 Schley street Newark New Jersey 07112.

I also want to keep you in prayers send me your prayer request

MIRACLE OF GOD MINISTRIES INC

343 Sanford avenue Newark
New Jersey 07106

Also send in your generous donation to support this work at
www.fnabaziehealingministries.org

CONCLUSION

"Let the beauty of what you love be what you do."

-Rumi

"Success is no accident. *It is hard work, perseverance, learning, studying, sacrifice* and most of all, love of what you are doing or learning to do."---**Pele**

"Work hard for what you want, because it won't come to you without a fight. You have *to be strong* and *courageous* and know that you can do anything you put your mind to. If somebody puts you down or criticizes you, just keep on believing in yourself and turn it into something positive."—**Leah LaBelle**

"Keep your *dreams alive*. Understand to achieve anything requires *faith and belief in yourself, vision, hard work, determination, and dedication.* Remember all things are

CHAPTER 2 : The Power of a Big Dream

possible for those who believe."-**Gail Devers**

"Success isn't always about greatness. *It's about consistency. Consistent hard work leads to success.* Greatness will come."-**Dwayne Johnson**

"The price of success is hard work, dedication to the job at hand, and the determination that whether we win or lose, we have applied the best of ourselves to the task at hand." –**Vincent Lombardi**

"Stay true to yourself, yet always be open to learn. Work hard, and never give up on your dreams, even when nobody else believes they can come true but you. These are not cliches but real tools you need no matter what you do in life to stay focused on your path."-**Phillip Sweet**

"A dream doesn't become reality through magic; it takes sweat, determination, and hard work." –**Colin Powell**

"Therefore if any man be in Christ, he is a new creature: old things are passed away; behold, all things are become new". **2cor5:17**

I encourage you to repent in prayers of any negative word you have ever spoken against your life and future. Speak the right word and make these confessions boldly in faith.

REPEAT THIS PRAYER AFTER ME....

"Say Lord Jesus, I accept you today, as my Lord and my savior, forgive me of my sins wash me with your blood. Right now, I believe, I am sanctified. I am save. I am free. I am free from the Power of sin to serve the Lord Jesus. Thank you Lord for saving me. Amen."

What must I do to determine my divine visitation?

CHAPTER 2 : The Power of a Big Dream

To determine divine visitation you must be born again! *The word says as many as received him, to them gave He power to become the sons of God. Even to them that believe on his name.*

To qualify for divine visitation do the following sincerely

1) Acknowledge that you are a sinner and that He died for you.Rom3:23.

2) Repent of your sins. Acts 3:19, Luke13:5, 2Peter3:9

3) Believe in your heart that Jesus died for your sin.Romans10:10

4) Confess Jesus as the Lord over your life. Romans10:10, Acts2:21

I really want to hear from you. You can join me if you are in the area to worship with us

Dream Big & Believe in Yourself

MIRACLE OF GOD MINISTRIES INC

343 SANFORD AVENUE NEWARK
NEW JERSEY 07106
Jesus is Lord!

EMAIL: Pastorfranknto@yahoo.com
Website www.fnabaziehealingministries.org

Please feel free to write me

REV FRANKLIN N ABAZIE
33 Schley street Newark
New Jersey 07112

CHAPTER 3
PRAYER OF SALVATION

"Neither is there salvation in any other: for there is none other name under heaven given among men, whereby we must be saved."

Acts4:12

There is only one name that will take us into heaven.

What must I do to determine my salvation?

To be saved-*we must be born again!* --- ***Then dream big and believe in your self***

To qualify for divine visitation do the following sincerely

1) Acknowledge that you are a sinner and that He died for you.Rom3:23.

2) Repent of your sins. Acts 3:19, Luke13:5, 2Peter3:9

3) Believe in your heart that Jesus died for your sin.Romans10:10

4) Confess Jesus as the Lord over your life. Romans10:10, Acts2:21

Are you saved?

If God have saved your life, speak to someone about Jesus. Disciple someone to join you worship the Lord Jesus Christ.

MIRACLE CARE OUTREACH

"…But that the members should have the same care one for another" 1cor12:25

We are all members of the body of Christ. Jesus commanded us to love our neighbor as ourselves. This includes caring for one another as a member of one body.

CHAPTER 3 : Prayer of Salvation

True love is expressed in caring and giving. The word says for God so Love He gave….

Reach out to someone in need of Jesus, help someone in crisis find Christ. Look out and prove your love to Jesus by caring and inviting your friends and associates to find Jesus the Healer.

Invite your friends to our Home Care Cell Fellowship (Miracle chapel Intl Satellite fellowship) In the USA at 33 Schley Street Newark New Jersey 07112.

If you are in Nigeria—**MIRACLE OF GOD MINISTRIES**

A.K.A"**MIRACLE CHAPEL INTL**" Mpama –Egbu-Owerri Imo state Nigeria.

(Home Care Cell fellowship Group). We meet every Tuesday at 6:00pm-7:00pm.

LIFE IS NOT ALL ABOUT DURATION BUT ITS ALL ABOUT DONATION

What does the above statement mean?....

Life consists not in accumulation of material wealth. (Luke12:15) But it's all about liberality....meaning- what you can give and share with others. Proverb11:25.

When you live for others--You live forever- because you out live your generation by the legacy you live behind after you depart into glory to be with the Lord. But when you live to yourself - you are reduced to self—you are easily forgotten when you die and depart in glory. Permit me to admonish you today to live your life to be a blessing to a soul connected to you today.

I want you to know that so many souls are connected and looking up to you, and through you so many souls will be saved and

CHAPTER 3 : Prayer of Salvation

rescued from destruction. Will you disciple someone today to find Jesus Christ?

As a genuine Christian; it is your duty to evangelize Jesus Christ to all you meet on your way. Jesus is still in the healing business-Jesus is still doing miracles from time of old to now. Therefore tell someone about Jesus Christ today, disciple and bring them to Church. John 1:45 *Philip findeth Nathanael....*

Please to prove the sincerity of your love for God today; please become a soul winner. The dignity of your Christianity is hidden in your boldness to proclaim and evangelize Jesus Christ to all you meet on your way. There is a question mark on the integrity of your Christianity until you become a life soul winner. Invite someone to join us worship the Lord Jesus this coming Sunday. **Amen**

Dream Big & Believe in Yourself

MIRACLE OF GOD MINISTRIES PILLARS OF THE COMMISSION

We Believe Preach and Practice the following

1) We believe and preach Salvation to every living human being

2) We believe and preach Repentance and forgiveness of sins

3) We believe and preach the baptism of the Holy Spirit and Spiritual gifts

4) We believe and teach the Prosperity

5) We believe and preach Divine Healing and Miracles (Signs &Wonder)

6) We believe and preach Faith

7) We believe and Proclaim the Power of God (Supernatural)

8) We believe and Proclaim Praise& Worship to God

CHAPTER 3 : Prayer of Salvation

9) We believe and preach Wisdom
10) We believe and preach Holiness (Consecration)
11) We believe and preach Vision
12) We believe and teach the Word of God
13) We believe and teach Success
14) We believe and practice Prayer
15) We believe and teach Deliverance

This 15 stones form the Pillars of Our Commission. Become part of this church family and follow this great move of God.

MY HEART FELT PRAYER FOR YOU

It is my prayer that you dream big and believe in yourself. I see you impacting your world. I see you making a difference. I see you breaking through. I see the Glory of God upon your life.

Now let me Pray for you:

My Father, My Father, Grant me the ability to *Dream big and believe in myself* in the Mighty Name of Jesus Christ.

THE POWER OF EVANGELISM

"Go ye therefore, and teach all nations, baptizing them in the name of the Father, and of the Son, and of the Holy Ghost:" **Mathew28:19**

Evangelism has power to attract the blessing of the Lord upon our lives. It is written "And ye shall serve the Lord your God, and he shall bless thy bread, and thy water; and I will take sickness away from the midst of thee." Exodus23:26.

Evangelizing, and bringing men and women to the cross of Jesus Christ is a great commandment. According to the above scripture, we are commanded to teach all nations, the name of Jesus Christ.

CHAPTER 3 : Prayer of Salvation

It is my prayer that you will witness the name of Jesus Christ to someone today.

Remember…………

"And they that be wise shall shine as the brightness of the firmament; and they that turn many to righteousness as the stars for ever and ever." **Daniel12:3**

OPERATION--"ONE MAN TEN MEN"

"Thus saith the Lord of hosts; In those days it shall come to pass, that ten men shall take hold out of all languages of the nations, even shall take hold of the skirt of him that is a Jew, saying, We will go with you: for we have heard that God is with you." **Zech 8:23**

If someone directed you to this ministry, it is divine wisdom for you to bring someone else also. If you googled to come into contact with us, I will recommend you also tell ten of your contacts and share with them what Jesus is doing through this ministry. Tell everybody about Jesus, also tell them to contact this ministry. Jesus is Lord!!

OPERATION ONE MAN ONE SOUL

If you cannot bring ten people at one time, at least you can talk to one person per time.

I recommend that you look for just one person who will respond positively and bring them to church. Or tell them about this ministry. That convert, is your own convert minister to them the love of Jesus Christ.

JESUS IS LORD!

CHAPTER 4
ABOUT THE AUTHOR

Rev Franklin N Abazie is the founding and Presiding Pastor of Miracle of God Ministries with headquarters in Newark, New Jersey USA and a branch church in Owerri- Imo State Nigeria. He is following the footsteps of one of his mentors, Oral Roberts (Healing Evangelist) of the blessed memory. The Lord passed Oral Roberts healing mantle two days before he went to be with the Lord at age 91 into the hand of healing evangelist-Rev Franklin N Abazie in a vision.

In all his services the Power and Presence of God is present to heal all in his audience. He is an ordained man of God with a Healing Ministry reviving the healing and miracle ministry of Jesus Christ of Nazareth.

Pastor Franklin N Abazie, is called by God with a unique mandate: **"THE MOMENT IS DUE TO IMPACT YOUR WORLD THROUGH THE REVIVAL OF THE HEALING & MIRACLE MINISTRY OF JESUS CHRIST OF NAZARETH**

I AM SENDING YOU TO RESTORE HEALTH UNTO THEE AND I WILL HEAL THEE OF THY WOUNDS. SAID THE LORD OF HOST"

He is a gifted ardent Teacher of the word of God who operates also in the office of a Prophet, generating and attracting undeniable signs & wonders, special miracles and healings, with apostolic fireworks of the Holy Ghost. He is the founding and presiding senior Pastor of this fast growing Healing ministry. He has written over 86 inspirational, healing and transforming books covering almost all aspect of divine healing and life. He is happily married and blessed with children.

BOOKS BY REV FRANKLIN N ABAZIE

1) Commanding Abundance
2) The outcome of faith
3) Understanding the secret of prevailing prayers.
4) Understanding the secret of the man God uses
5) Activating my due Season
6) Overcoming Divine Verdicts
7) The Outcome of Divine Wisdom
8) Understanding God's Restoration Mandate
9) Walking in the Victory and Authority of the truth
10) Gods Covenant Exemption
11) Destiny Restoration Pillars
12) Provoking Acceptable Praise

13) Understanding Divine Judgment
14) Activating Angelic Re-enforcement
15) Provoking Un-Merited Favor
16) The Benefits of the Speaking faith
17) Understanding Divine Arrangement
18) Understanding Divine Healing
19) The Mystery of Endurance
20) Obeying Divine Instructions
21) Understanding the Voice of God
22) Never give up on Hope
23) The prevailing Power of faith
24) Understanding Divine Prosperity
25) The Reward of Prayer
26) Covenant Keys to Answered Prayers
27) Activating the Forces of Vengeance
28) Put your faith to work
29) Where is your trust?

30) The Audacity of the Blood of Jesus
31) Redeeming Your Days
32) The Force of Vision
33) Breaking the shackles of Family curses
34) Wisdom for Marriage Stability
35) Overcoming prevailing challenges
36) The Prayer solution
39) The power of Prayer
40) Prayer strategy
41) The prayer that works
42) Walking in Forgiveness
43) The Power of the grace of God
44) The Power of Persistence
45) The benefit of the speaking faith.
46) Fearless faith
47) Redeeming Your Days.
48) The Supernatural Power of Prophecy

49) The companionship of the Holy Spirit
50) Understanding Divine Judgement
51) Understanding Divine Prosperity
52) Dominating Controlling Forces
53) The winner's Faith
54) Destiny Restoration Pillars
55) Developing Spiritual Muscles
56) Inexplicable faith
57) The lifestyle of Prayer
58) Developing a positive attitude in life.
59) The Mystery of Divine supply
60) Encounter with the Power of God
61) Walking in love
62) Praying in the Spirit
63) How to provoke your testimony
64) Walking in the reality of the anointing
65) The Reality of new birth

Books By Rev Franklin N Abazie

66) The Price of freedom
67) The Supernatural Power of faith
68) The intellectual components of Redemption.
69) Overcoming Fear
70) Overcoming Prevailing Challenges
71) My life & Ministry
72) The Mystery of Praise
73) Dream Big and believe in yourself
74) Christin Character Builder
75) The Power of Bold Declaration
76) The Power of Discipline & Dedication

MIRACLE OF GOD MINISTRIES

NIGERIA CRUSADE
2012

MIRACLE OF GOD MINISTRIES

NIGERIA CRUSADE
2012

MIRACLE OF GOD MINISTRIES

*NIGERIA CRUSADE
2012*

Wisdom Center-
Forth-Worth Texas
Pastors Conference
2017

www.ingramcontent.com/pod-product-compliance
Lightning Source LLC
Chambersburg PA
CBHW020126130526
44591CB00032B/551